Preparing for KREUTZER

(Published in Two Volumes)

An Intermediate Course of Violin Study
Based on the Famous Works of Kayser, Mazas,
Dont, De Beriot, Dancla, Blumenstengel, and
Other Masters of the Violin Repertoire

by HARVEY S. WHISTLER

Copyright MCMLII by Rubank, Inc., Chicago, Illinois
International Copyright Secured — Printed in U.S.A.

For DAILY PRACTICE and for REVIEW

COMPREHENSIVE COURSE OF STUDY

EXERCISES FOR DAILY PRACTICE

		Page
Developing Bowing	Whistler	4
Etude for Developing Bowing	Ševčík	5
Developing Trilling	Whistler	6
Developing Fingerboard Facility	Schöen	7
Developing Technic in Thirds	Schradieck	38
Developing Technic in Sixths	Schradieck	39
Developing Technic in Octaves	Schradieck	40
Developing Artistry in Bowing	Casorti	50

EXERCISES FOR REVIEW

Advanced Position Playing	Schradieck	22
Cadenza Playing	Dancla	23
Staccato Playing	De Beriot	27
Dynamic Playing	Whistler	51

ETUDES IN MINOR KEYS

Etude in A Minor	Blumenstengel	8
Etude in E Minor	Dont	9
Etude in B Minor	Kayser	10
Etude in D Minor	Dont	11
Etude in G Minor	Mazas	12
Etude in F# Minor	Weiss	13
Etude in C# Minor	Böhmer	14
Etude in C Minor	Dont	15
Etude in F Minor	Kayser	16
Chromatic Caprice	Sitt	17

SELECTED STUDIES

Arpeggio Artistry	Kayser	18
String-Skipping Study No. 1	Mazas	20
String-Skipping Study No. 2	Campagnoli	21
Cadenza Studies, Nos. 1, 2, and 3	Meerts	24
Cadenza Caprice	Dancla	25
Art of Cross-Fingering	Alard	26
Staccato Study No. 1	Kayser	28
Staccato Study No. 2	Dancla	30
Staccato Study No. 3	Mazas	31
Bow-Art Caprice No. 1	Kayser	32
Bow-Art Caprice No. 2	Dont	33
Position Prelude	Kayser	34
Perpetuúm Mobile	Kayser	36
Artist's Chromatic Caprice No. 1	Spohr	46
Artist's Chromatic Caprice No. 2	Depas	48

ADVANCED ETUDES IN DOUBLE-STOPS

Tremolo Bowing in Double-Stops	Mazas	41
Artist's Etude No. 1 in Double-Stops	Dont	42
Artist's Etude No. 2 in Double-Stops	Dont	43
Artist's Etude in Chords	Dont	44
Artist's Etude in Octaves	Wohlfahrt	45

CONCERT CAPRICES

Caprice d'Artiste	Mazas	52
Caprice de Virtuosité	Mazas	53
Caprice Brillante	Mazas	54
Capriccio Concertante	Mazas	55
Fantaisie de Concert	Mazas	56

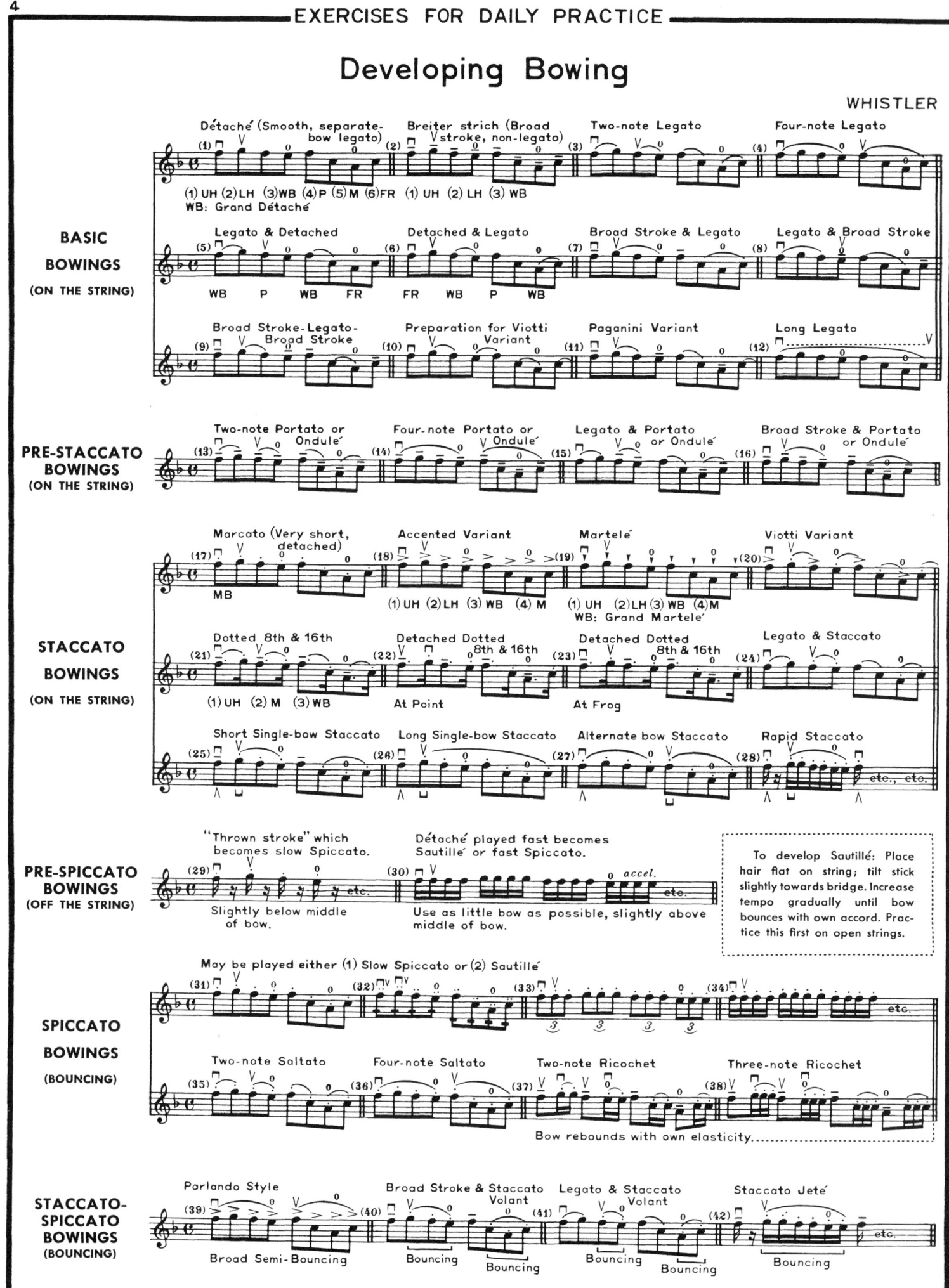

EXERCISES FOR DAILY PRACTICE

Etude for Developing Bowing

ŠEVČÍK, Op. 2

To be memorized. All bowing variants of opposite page should be systematically applied to this etude.

Developing Trilling

WHISTLER

Play as many notes as possible in each trill. Raise fingers with a rapid, light action, just high enough to clear the string being played upon.

Also practice sustaining each trill for (1) eight counts, and (2) sixteen counts.

Also practice starting with the auxiliary note and sustaining each trill for (1) four counts, (2) eight counts, and (3) sixteen counts. Also practice in the manner of Preparatory Studies, as shown on page 36, Vol. I.

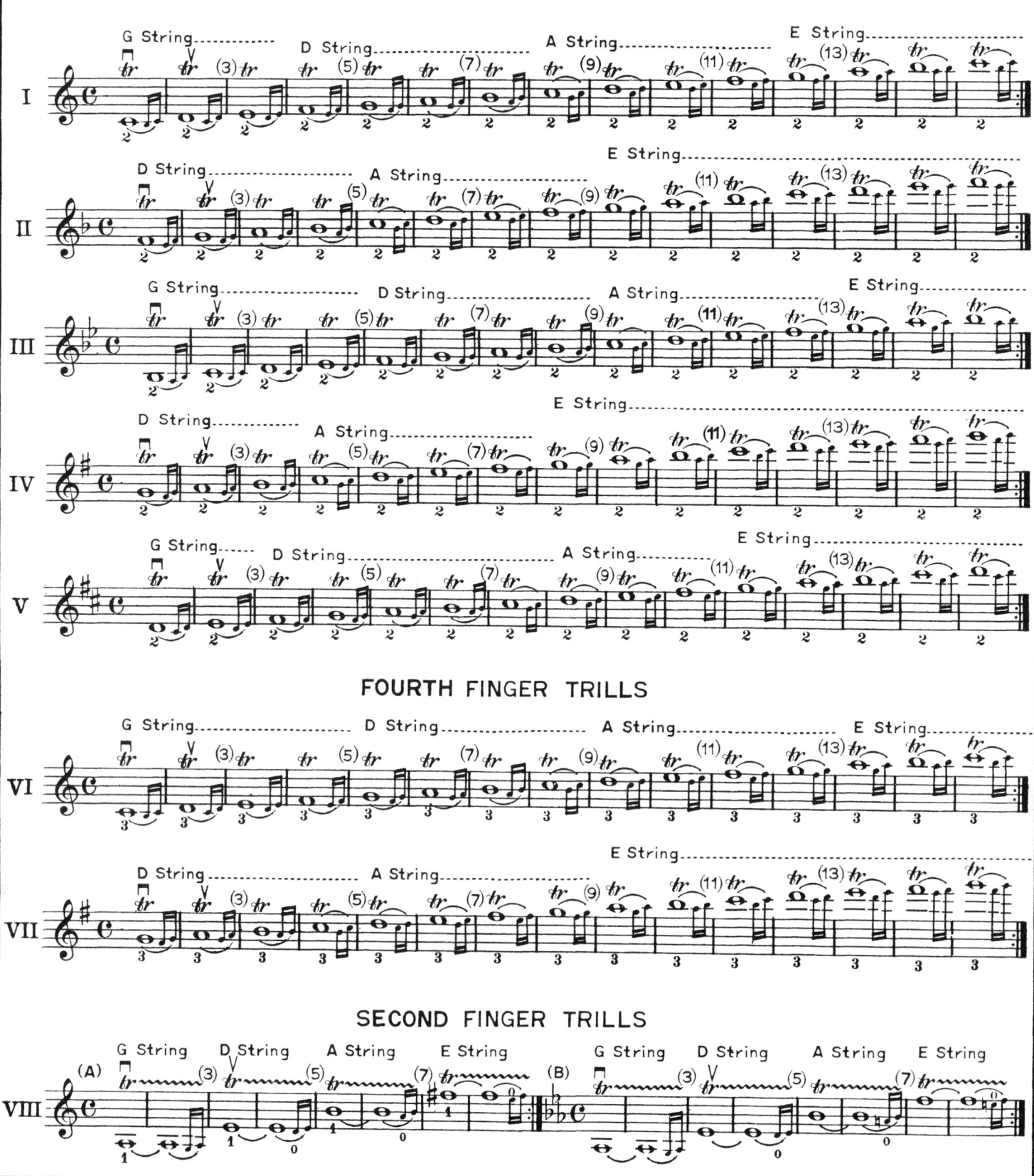

EXERCISES FOR DAILY PRACTICE

Developing Fingerboard Facility

SCHÖEN, Op. 38

Practice slowly at first. Later increase speed, raising fingers with a rapid, light action.
⌢4 : Extend fourth finger while hand remains in same position.

(NATURAL - FLAT ARPEGGI)

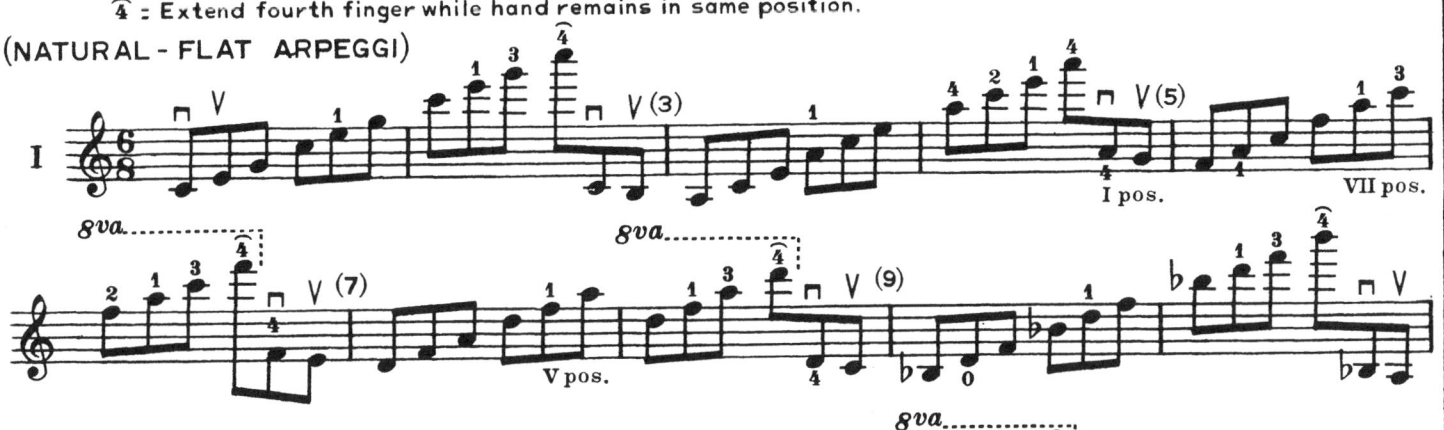

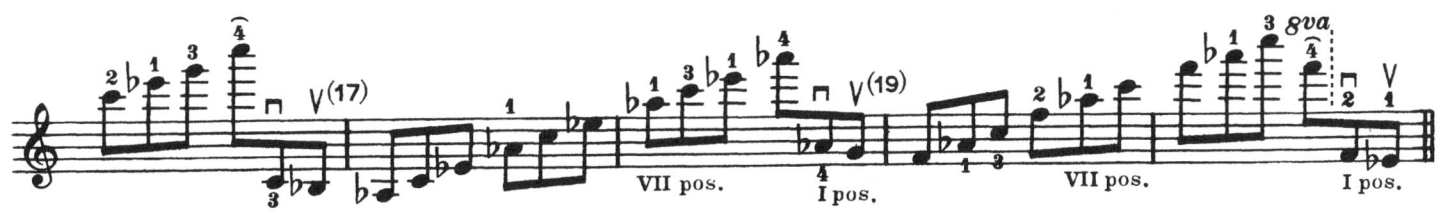

(SHARP - NATURAL ARPEGGI)

* All fingerings are optional. Teachers should substitute their own fingerings when they are better suited for their needs.

** Numbers within brackets suggest alternate styles of finger-technic.

Etudes in Minor Keys
Etude in A Minor

BLUMENSTENGEL, Op. 33

To be played in a firm, forceful manner. Shifting should be smooth and inaudible.

Etude in E Minor

DONT, Op. 37

To be played with broad strokes of the bow.

Also practice using (1) détaché bowings, as well as other basic variants, (2) selected staccato variants, and (3) selected spiccato variants.

Etude in B Minor

KAYSER, Op. 20

To be played using (1) slow spiccato bowing and (2) sautillé bowing.
Also practice using other spiccato variants.

Etude in D Minor

DONT, Op. 37

To be played in a firm, forceful manner. Notes indicated marcato (♪) should be short and crisp.

Etude in G Minor

MAZAS, Op. 36

To be played strictly in time. When playing the quadruplet figuration the fingers should be raised with a rapid, light action.

Etude in F# Minor

WEISS, Op. 80

The dotted eighth note should be broad in effect, and the sixteenth note that follows, short and abrupt.

Etude in C# Minor

BÖHMER, Op. 54

To be played in a broad, forceful style, with sweeping strokes of the bow. Shifting of positions should be inaudible.

Etude in C Minor

DONT, Op. 37

To be played in a firm, forceful manner. Notes indicated marcato (♪) should be short and crisp. Legato passages should be smooth and connected. String transfers should be inaudible.

Etude in F Minor

KAYSER, Op. 20

Chromatic Caprice

ASCENDING FINGER PATTERN:
0-1-1-2-2-3-4

DESCENDING FINGER PATTERN:
4-3-2-2-1-1-0

SITT, Op. 32

Practice slowly at first. Maintain a steady tempo throughout. Also practice using a separate bow for each note.

Selected Studies
Arpeggio Artistry

KAYSER, Op. 20

Keep fingers down as long as possible. All string transfers should be smooth throughout. Maintain a steady tempo at all times.

String-Skipping Study No.1

MAZAS, Op. 36

To be played strictly in marcato style. Strings passed over should not be touched with the bow at the time of transfer.

String-Skipping Study No. 2

CAMPAGNOLI, Op. 21

To be played strictly in marcato style. Strings passed over should not be touched with the bow at the time of transfer.

EXERCISES FOR REVIEW

Advanced Position Playing

SCHRADIECK
from the
TECHNICAL VIOLIN SCHOOL

Also practice (1) using a separate bow for each note, and (2) slurring each complete measure.

Remain in each position until a change is indicated.

EXERCISES FOR REVIEW
Cadenza Playing
TRIPLET FIGURATION

DANCLA, Op. 164

To be played in smooth, legato style. Shifting should be inaudible.

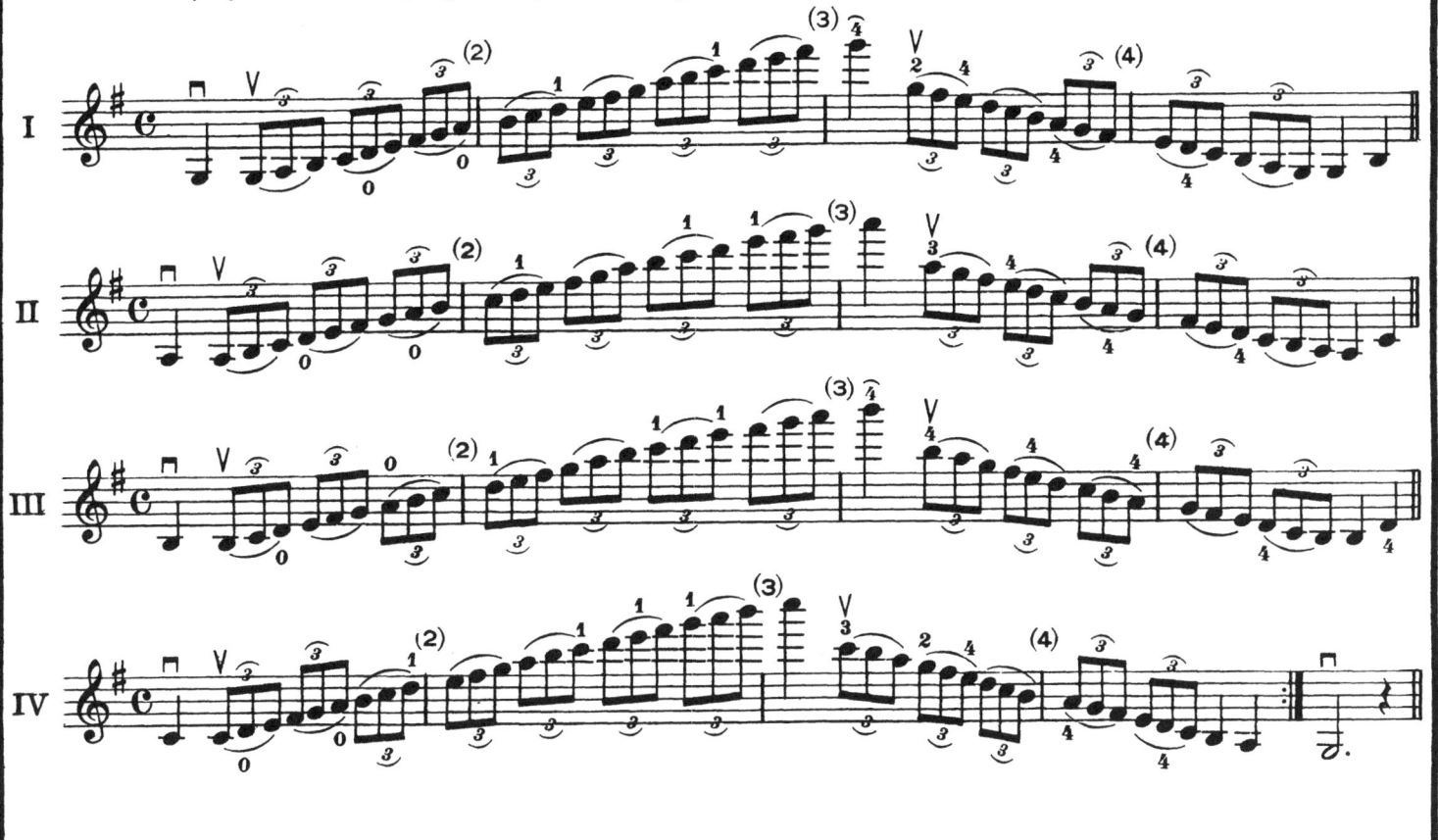

QUADRUPLET FIGURATION

DANCLA, Op. 164

To be played in smooth, legato style. Shifting should be inaudible.

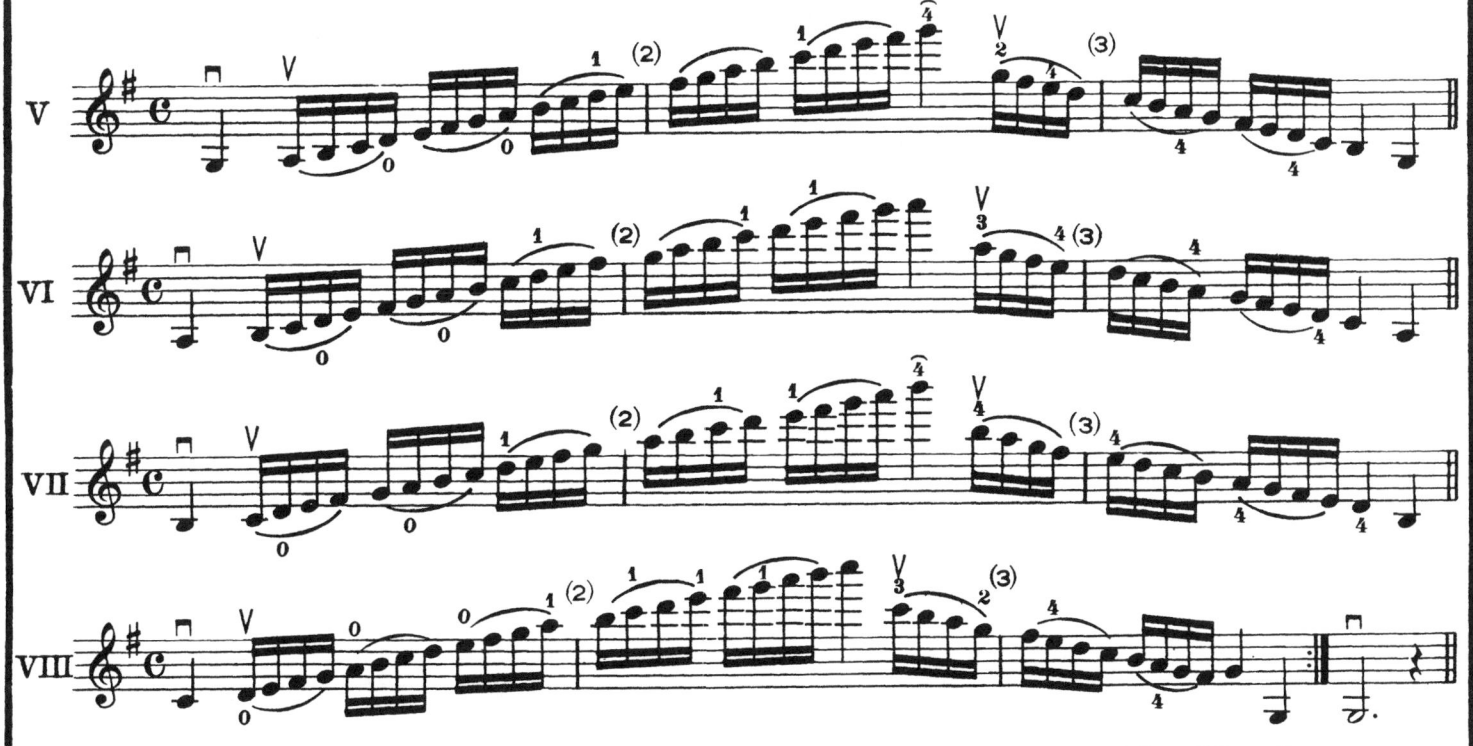

Cadenza Study No. 1

MEERTS
from the
ARTISTS' MECHANISM OF THE VIOLIN

Brackets and illustrate manner of grouping tones.

Practice slowly at first, being careful to use fingering and bowing as indicated.

Cadenza Study No. 2

MEERTS
from the
ARTISTS' MECHANISM OF THE VIOLIN

Practice slowly at first, being careful to use fingering and bowing as indicated.

Cadenza Study No. 3

MEERTS
from the
ARTISTS' MECHANISM OF THE VIOLIN

Practice slowly at first, being careful to use fingering and bowing as indicated.

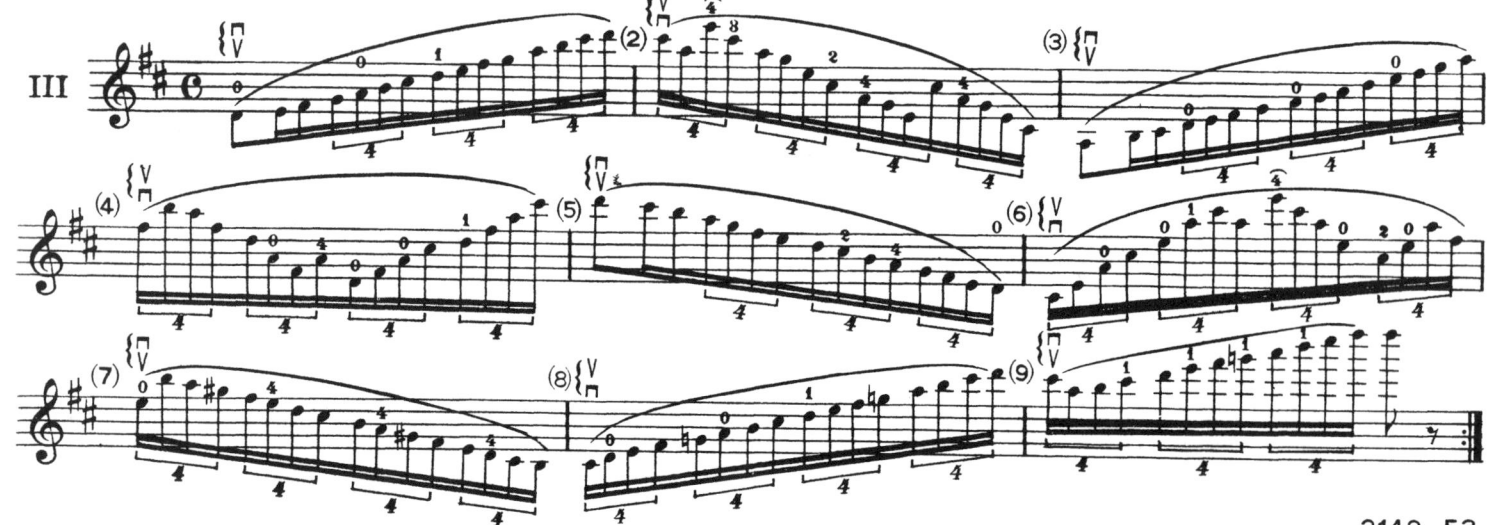

2142-53

Cadenza Caprice

DANCLA, Op. 52

Brackets ⌐3⌐ and ⌐4⌐ illustrate manner of grouping tones.
Practice cadenzas slowly at first, being careful to use fingering and bowing as indicated.

Art of Cross-Fingering

ALARD
from the
CONSERVATORY METHOD

⌣ = Draw back finger while hand remains in same position.

Also practice (1) using a separate bow for each note, and (2) slurring each complete measure.

EXERCISES FOR REVIEW
Staccato Playing

If difficulty is encountered in playing staccato, the performer should turn at once to the section devoted to that phase of violin technic in the comprehensive work, STACCATO AND SPICCATO, by Harvey S. Whistler, and begin a thorough study of such bowing.

ASCENDING STACCATO
DE BERIOT, Op. 102

Practice slowly at first. Gradually increase the speed. Each tone should be played in an abrupt, crisp manner.

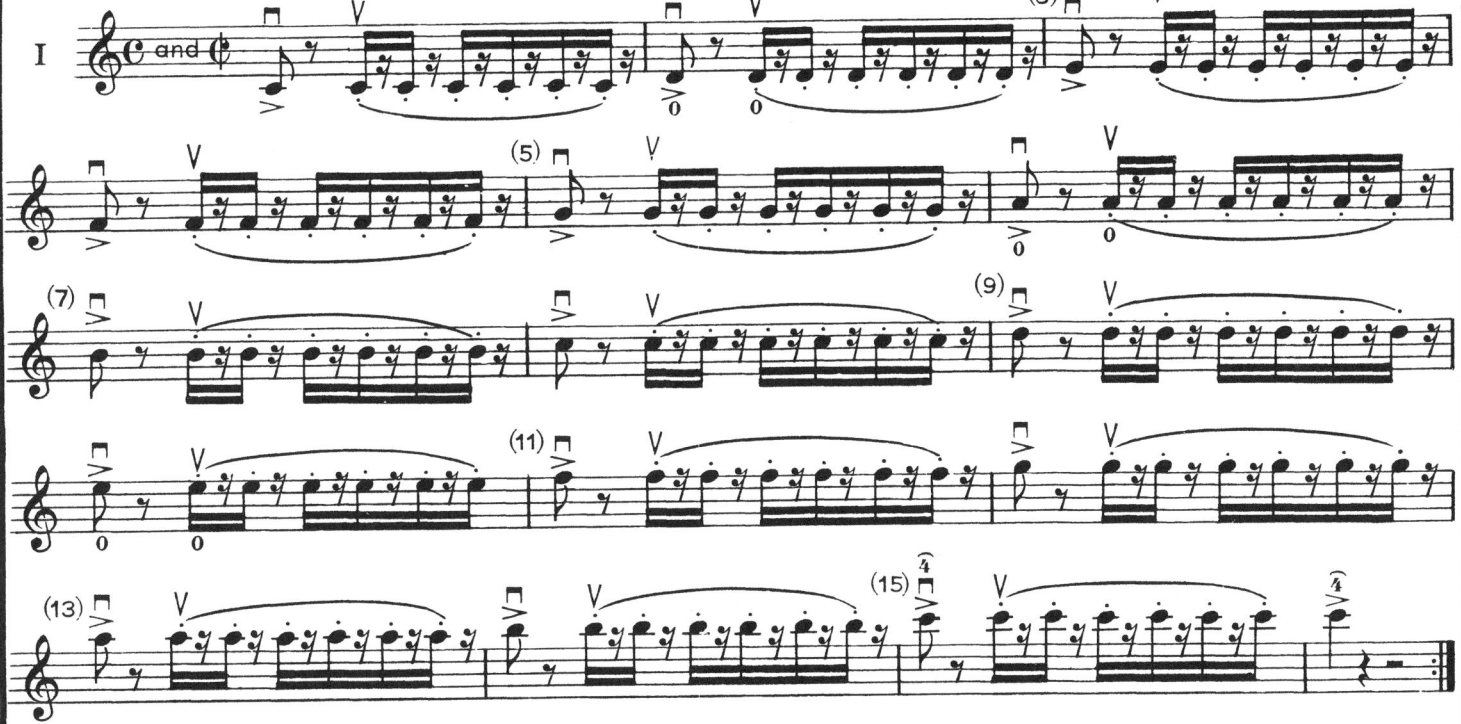

DESCENDING STACCATO
DE BERIOT, Op. 102

Practice slowly at first. Gradually increase the speed. Each tone should be played in an abrupt, crisp manner.

Staccato Study No. 1

KAYSER, Op. 20

Play the staccato notes in an abrupt, crisp manner. Each tone should be clear, but short, and with individual emphasis on it.

Staccato Study No. 2

DANCLA, Op. 52

Play the staccato notes in an abrupt, crisp manner. Each tone should be clear, but short, and with individual emphasis on it.

Staccato Study No. 3

MAZAS, Op. 36

Play the staccato notes in an abrupt, crisp manner. Each tone should be clear, but short, and with individual emphasis on it.

Bow-Art Caprice No. 1

KAYSER, Op. 20

Bow-Art Caprice No. 2

DONT, Op. 37

Position Prelude

KAYSER, Op. 20

Also practice using (1) Détaché bowings, as well as other basic variants, (2) selected staccato variants, and (3) selected spiccato variants.

Perpetuúm Mobile

KAYSER, Op. 20

Practice slowly at first. Later increase the tempo, using a rapid, light finger action.

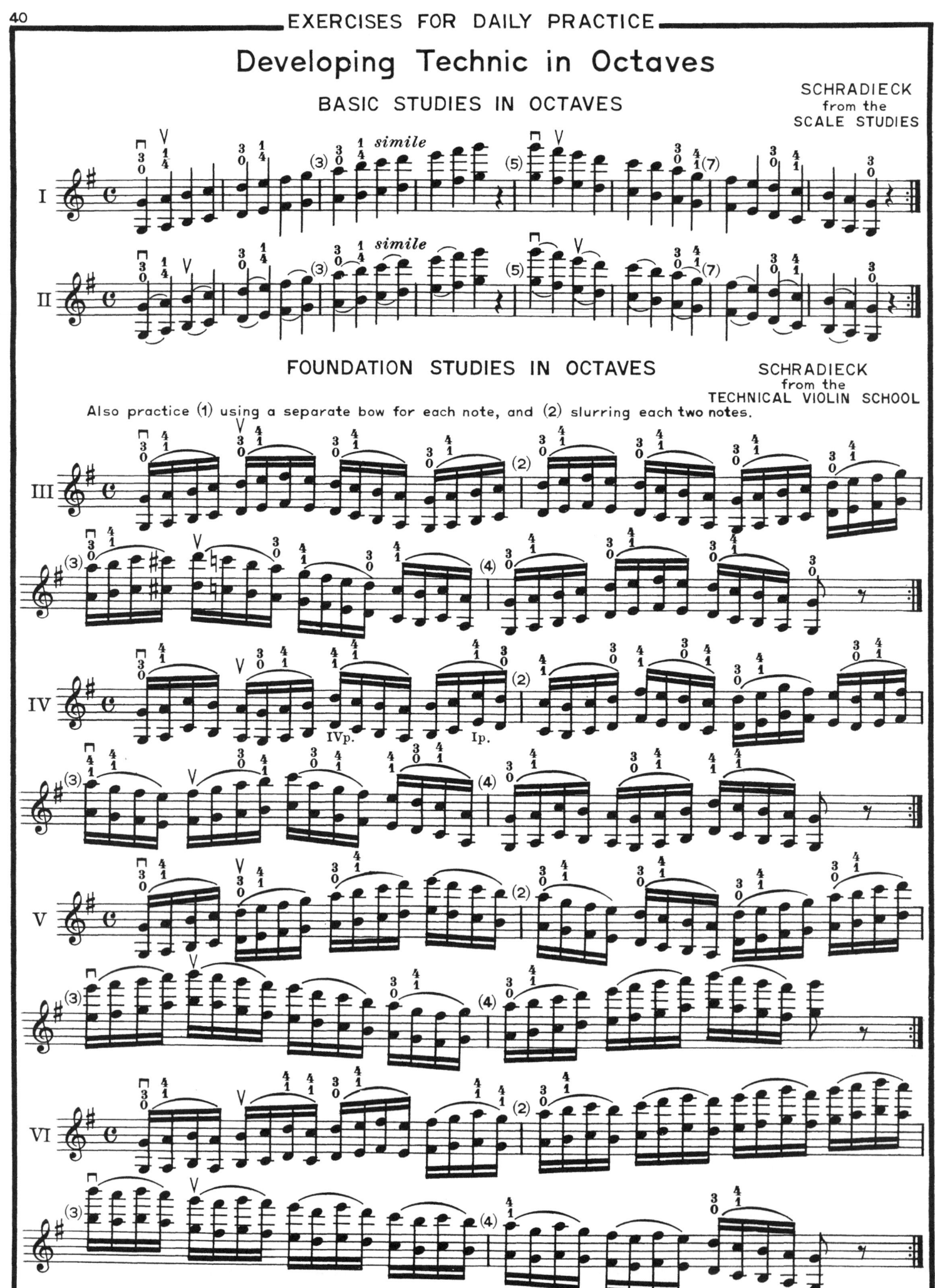

Advanced Etudes in Double-Stops
Tremolo Bowing in Double-Stops

MAZAS, Op. 36

When playing tremolo bowing, keep the bow on the string at all times. Do not bounce the bow.

Artist's Etude No. 1 in Double-Stops

DONT, Op. 37

Practice slowly at first. Play individual measures as exercises, repeating them until the difficulties contained therein are reduced to a minimum.

Artist's Etude No. 2 in Double-Stops

DONT, Op. 37

Practice slowly at first. Play individual measures as exercises, repeating them until the difficulties contained therein are reduced to a minimum.

Artist's Etude in Chords

DONT, Op. 37

In order to test intonation, first play lower and middle tones together, immediately tilting the bow and playing the middle and upper tones together. Gradually the tones of the three-note chords should be played simultaneously.

Artist's Etude in Octaves

WOHLFAHRT, Op. 45

Practice slowly. Do not proceed from one octave to the next until the intonation is correct.

Artist's Chromatic Caprice No. 1

ASCENDING FINGER PATTERN:
0 - 1 - 1 - 2 - 2 - 3 - 4

DESCENDING FINGER PATTERN:
4 - 3 - 2 - 2 - 1 - 1 - 0

SPOHR
from the
VIOLIN SCHOOL

Practice slowly at first. Maintain a steady tempo throughout.

Artist's Chromatic Caprice No. 2

* ASCENDING FINGER PATTERN:
 0-1-1-2-2-3-4
* DESCENDING FINGER PATTERN:
 4-3-2-2-1-1-0

DEPAS, Op. 105

Practice slowly at first. Maintain a steady tempo throughout.

Also practice using a separate bow for each note.

* Alternate fingering is written in parentheses below the staff.

Exercises for Daily Practice

Developing Artistry in Bowing

"FOUR-MINUTE" SOSTENUTO ETUDE

CASORTI
from the
TECHNIC OF THE BOW

Save as much bow as possible. Each bow eventually should be held for duration of ONE MINUTE!
Also practice starting up-bow.

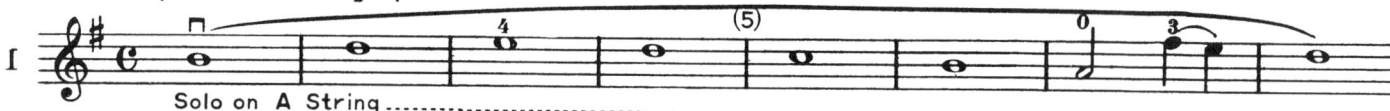
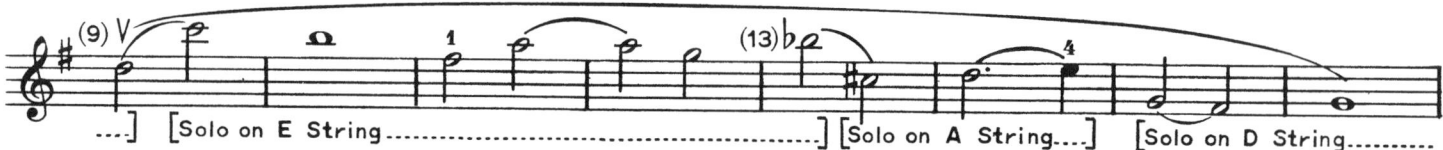
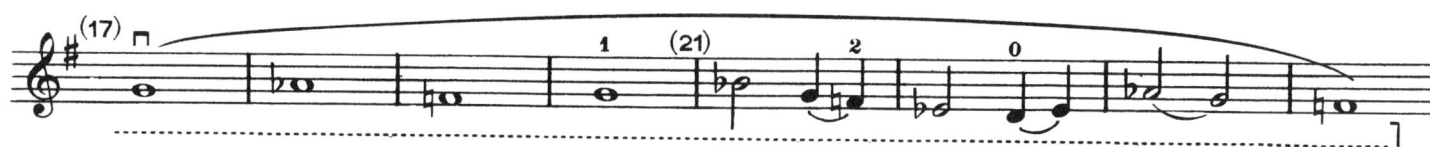
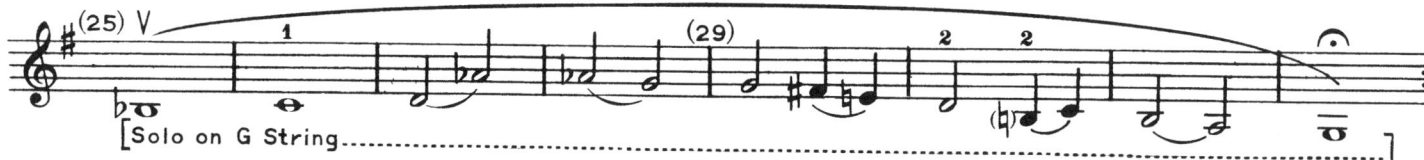

LEGATO CAPRICE

CASORTI
from the
TECHNIC OF THE BOW

Keep fingers down as long as possible. All string transfers should be smooth throughout.

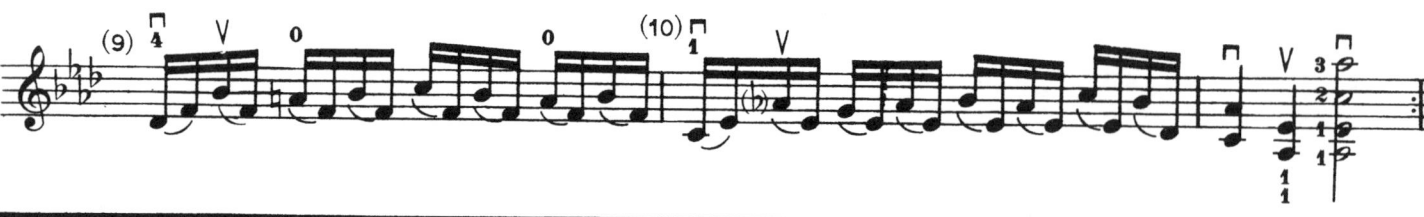

EXERCISES FOR REVIEW
Dynamic Playing

WHISTLER

Also practice sustaining each CRESCENDO, DIMINUENDO and CRESCENDO-DIMINUENDO for (1) eight counts and (2) sixteen counts.

Also apply the dynamic progressions below to other major and minor scale patterns.

Concert Caprices
Caprice d' Artiste
(Solo)

MAZAS, Op. 36

Caprice de Virtuosité
(Solo)

MAZAS, Op. 36

Caprice Brillante
(Solo)

MAZAS, Op. 36

Capriccio Concertante
(Solo for G String)

MAZAS, Op. 36

Fantaisie de Concert
(Solo)

MAZAS, Op. 36